Pebble® Plus

Understanding Differences

Some Kids Are
Blind

Revised Edition

Lola M Schaefer

raintree

a Capstone company — publishers for children

Raintree is an imprint of Capstone Global Library Limited, a company incorporated in England and Wales having its registered office at 264 Banbury Road, Oxford, OX2 7DY – Registered company number: 6695582

www.raintree.co.uk
myorders@raintree.co.uk

Editorial credits
Sarah Bennett, designer; Tracy Cummins, media researcher; Laura Manthe, production specialist

Photo credits
Capstone Studio: Karon Dubke, 5, 9; Getty Images: BLOOM image, 19, Majdi Fathi/NurPhoto, 21, mapodile, 7, Richard Hutchings, 17; Science Source: Amélie Benoist Khakurel, 13, Lawrence Migdale, Cover; Shutterstock: wavebreakmedia, 11; SuperStock: Spencer Grant/age fotostock, 15

Printed and bound in India.

ISBN 978 1 4747 5687 7
22 21 20 19 18
10 9 8 7 6 5 4 3 2 1

British Library Cataloguing in Publication Data
A full catalogue record for this book is available from the British Library.

Contents

Blindness

Some kids are blind.

Kids who are blind

cannot see.

Some kids are blind
when they are born.
Some kids become
blind from an illness
or from getting injured.

Kids who are blind use their other senses. They hear their friends talking on the phone. They feel things around them.

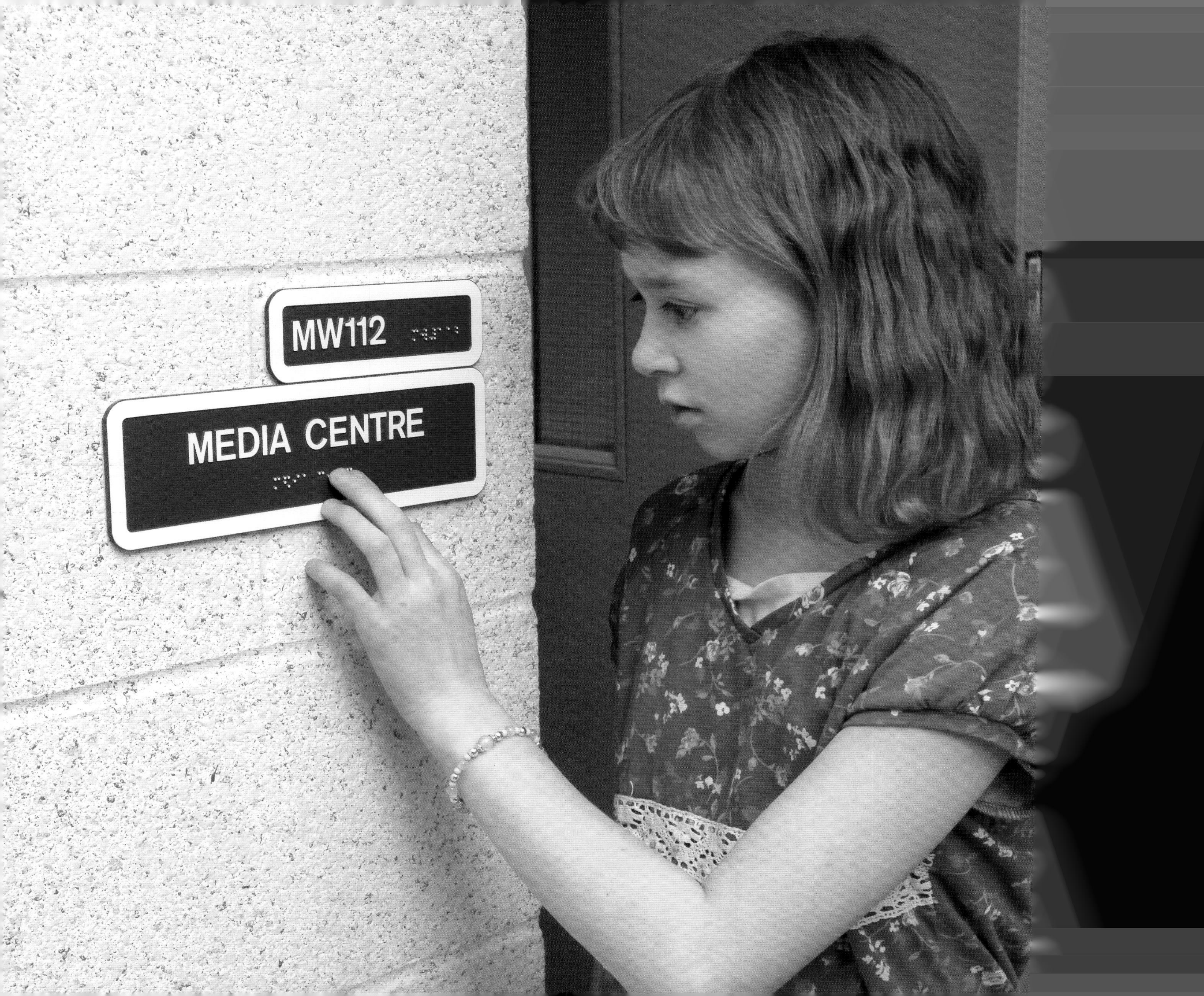
MW112
MEDIA CENTRE

Braille

Some kids who are blind read Braille. Braille is raised dots that stand for letters and numbers.

Some kids who are blind use Braille computers to do homework and send email.

Everyday life

Some kids who are blind use white canes to guide them.

Adults who are blind

can use guide dogs.

Some kids who are blind enjoy listening to audiobooks.

Some kids who are blind
like to do karate.

Glossary

audiobook recording of someone reading a book aloud

blind unable to see or having very limited sight; some people who are blind can see light and colour

Braille set of raised dots that stand for letters and numbers; people use their fingertips to read the raised dots; Louis Braille of France invented Braille in the early 1800s

guide dog dog that is specially trained to lead adults who are blind; guide dogs help adults who are blind to move safely in public places

senses ways of learning about your surroundings; hearing, smelling, touching, tasting and seeing are the five senses

Find out more

Books

Having a Disability (Questions and Feelings About), Louise Spilsbury (Franklin Watts, 2017)

We All Have Different Abilities (Celebrating Differences), Melissa Higgins (Raintree, 2017)

Websites

Find out what it's like to live with a disabled brother: https://www.bbc.co.uk/education/clips/ztbfb9q

Information about living with a disabled sibling: https://www.sibs.org.uk/

A charity that helps improve the lives of children who use wheelchairs: http://www.whizz-kidz.org.uk/about-us

Comprehension questions

1. What is Braille? How does it help people who are blind?

2. How does a person who is blind use his or her other senses?

3. How would using a cane be helpful to a person who is blind?

Index